Resilience S

REAL

I0005050

Commissioned by the **Cybersecurity** and **Infrastructure Security Agency**
Written by **Clint Watts** and **Farid Haque**

Resilience Series

REAL

CLINT WATTS

FARID HAQUE

ISBN 978-1-4341-0468-7

This book is made available in electronic form by the CISA, the Cybersecurity and Infrastructure Security Agency, which is a standalone United States federal agency, an operational component under Department of Homeland Security oversight. Its activities are a continuation of the National Protection and Programs Directorate:

https://www.cisa.gov/

As a U.S. government publication, this book is in the public domain.

This printed edition is published by Waking Lion Press, an imprint of the Editorium. Waking Lion Press is not endorsed by or affiliated in any way with the CISA or the U.S. Department of Homeland Security.

Waking Lion Press™ and Editorium™ are trademarks of:

The Editorium, LLC
West Jordan, UT 84081-6132
www.editorium.com

The views expressed in this book are the responsibility of the authors and do not necessarily represent the position of Waking Lion Press. The reader alone is responsible for the use of any ideas or information provided by this book.

This book is a work of fiction. The characters, places, and incidents in it are the products of the author's imagination or are represented fictitiously. Any resemblance of characters to actual persons is coincidental.

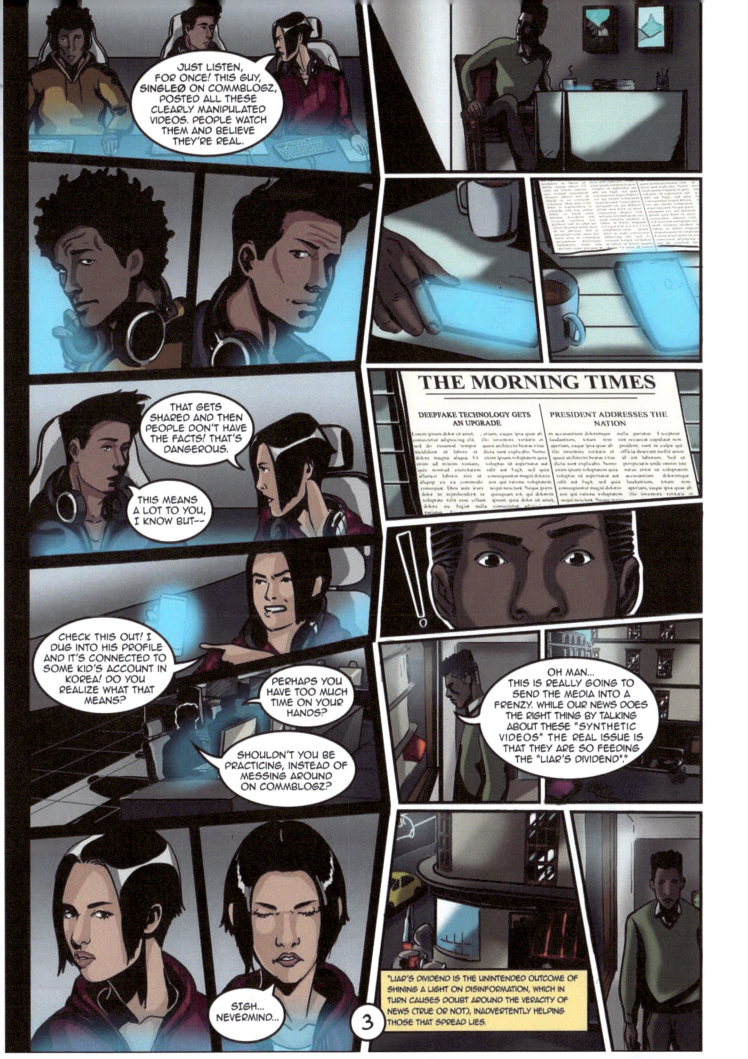

OK... TIME TO GET MR. CHAIRMAN ON THE LINE...

CommBlogz

Deepfakes

DEEPFAKE REQUEST MEGATHREAD

CELEBRITY DEEPFAKES THREAD(NSFW)

PHONEBOOK

Harry. D
Wilson. H
Steven. B
Johnny. D
Aiden. P
Andrew. W
Tyler. N
Hanzo. H

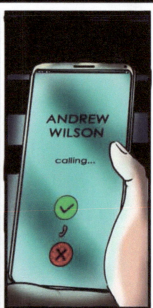

ANDREW WILSON

calling...

6

COULD I GET A 30 MIN APPOINTMENT WITH THE CHAIRMAN, RIGHT NOW?

IT'S A BIT SHORT NOTICE! BUT I AM SURE HE COULD SQUEEZE YOU IN CONSIDERING YOU'RE HIS FAVORITE NIECE!

THANK YOU, I WANTED TO GET YOUR TAKE ON THIS. MORE OF THESE DEEPFAKE VIDEOS ARE SHOWING UP ON COMMBLOGZ AND FINDING THEIR WAY TO OTHER SOCIAL MEDIA SITES. GOT INTO IT WITH A TROLL THERE YESTERDAY. IT SEEMS TO BE GETTING WORSE!

FIRST OFF, YOU SHOULDN'T ARGUE WITH TROLLS. HOW MANY TIMES HAVE I TOLD YOU THAT?

SECOND, YOU ARE CORRECT. THE TECH BEHIND THESE ALTERED VIDEOS IS GETTING MORE ADVANCED AND THE HARDWARE CHEAPER. DEEPFAKES USED TO BE THE PURVIEW OF A FEW. DID YOU EVER SEE THAT DEEPFAKE MY ALMA MATER MADE FOR NIXON'S ALTERNATIVE MOON LANDING VIDEO. IT'S AN INSTANT CLASSIC...

NOWADAYS THANKS TO THE LOW COST OF GPUS, JUST ABOUT ANYONE HAS THE PROCESSING POWER TO MAKE DEEPFAKES... OR, AS WE CALL THESE LOW BUDGET VERSIONS, CHEAP FAKES.

YEAH, BUT—

THIS IS SCARY, ESPECIALLY IN AN ELECTION YEAR! ALL THIS IS BEING DONE TO UNDERMINE OUR DEMOCRACY. THIS HAS MOSCOW WRITTEN ALL OVER IT!

*GPUS IS THE ACRONYM USED TO DESCRIBE GRAPHICS PROCESSING UNITS WHICH ARE SPECIALIZED, ELECTRONIC CIRCUITS DESIGNED TO RAPIDLY MANIPULATE AND ALTER MEMORY FOR A HARDWARE DEVICE TO ACCELERATE THE CREATION OF IMAGES. THEY ARE OFTEN USED TO IMPROVE PERFORMANCE FOR PERSONAL COMPUTERS, WORKSTATIONS, AND GAME CONSOLES (AS WELL AS OTHER DEVICES) THAT NEED TO DEAL WITH LARGE IMAGE RELATED DATA.

MAYBE IT'S TIME WE DUG DEEPER. I CAN TELL YOU A LITTLE MORE ABOUT DEEPFAKE TECHNOLOGY BEFORE I HAVE TO GO.

THE TERM "DEEPFAKE," A COMBINATION OF "DEEP LEARNING" AND "FAKE," IS USED TO DESCRIBE SYNTHETIC VIDEO OR AUDIO CONTENT, WHICH IS OFTEN CREATED WITH MALICIOUS INTENT TO SPREAD MIS AND/OR DISINFORMATION. THE TERM WAS FIRST USED BY A REDDIT USER IN 2017.

THE FIRST DEEPFAKES THAT GAINED NOTORIETY WERE MOSTLY FOCUSED ON NON-CONSENSUAL PORNOGRAPHY, CREATING SYNTHETIC MEDIA, OFTEN USING CELEBRITIES AS SUBJECTS, TO GARNER WIDESPREAD SHARING. IN MANY CASES THE SYNTHETIC MEDIA HAS BEEN USED AS A WAY TO SHAME, HUMILIATE, AND MANIPULATE VICTIMS AROUND THE WORLD. TECHNIQUES HAVE RANGED FROM FACE-SWAPPING TECHNOLOGY TO MUCH MORE COMPLEX APPLICATIONS.

THE TECHNOLOGY IS REPORTED TO HAVE EMERGED INITIALLY FROM ACADEMIC RESEARCH AT THE UNIVERSITY OF CALIFORNIA – BERKELEY AND WAS REFINED BY COMPUTER VISION EXPERTS IN SILICON VALLEY. THE MAJOR BREAKTHROUGH IS ATTRIBUTED TO A PAPER PUBLISHED BY A TEAM AT BERKELEY TITLED "VIDEO REWRITE: DRIVING VISUAL SPEECH WITH AUDIO." IN THIS PAPER, THE TEAM FOCUSED ON THE IMPORTANCE OF SYNCING LIP MOVEMENTS AND SPEECH AT A TIME WHEN MUCH OF APPLIED ARTIFICIAL INTELLIGENCE IN THE SPACE OF MACHINE LEARNING WAS LARGELY THEORETICAL.

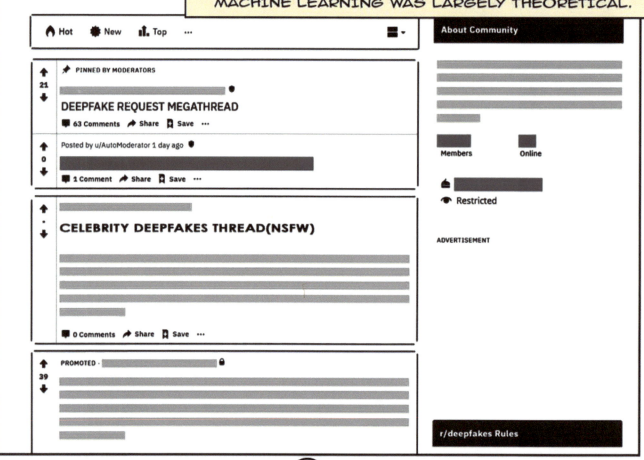

DEEPFAKES HAVE COME BY WAY OF NOT ONLY VIDEO BUT AUDIO TOO. THE ABILITY TO USE READILY AVAILABLE AND AFFORDABLE SOFTWARE TO CREATE FAKE SOUND OR VIDEO HAS BECOME AVAILABLE TO THE MASSES AS THE COST OF GRAPHICAL PROCESSING UNITS HAS FALLEN AND THE NECESSARY PROCESSING POWER TO MAKE A DEEPFAKE, WHICH WAS ONCE OUT OF REACH, HAS BECOME MORE ACCESSIBLE.

ACADEMICS HAVE ALSO BEEN HARD AT WORK SHOWCASING THE EXTENT TO WHICH DEEPFAKES CAN BE USED TO INFLUENCE MAINSTREAM MEDIA. MIT PRODUCED A VIDEO OF PRESIDENT RICHARD NIXON WHERE THEY PLAYED OUT AN ALTERNATIVE MOON LANDING STORY. THAT DEEPFAKE WAS USING A PRESIDENT OF YESTERDAY... FAST FORWARD TO AN ELECTION YEAR AND IMAGINE HOW VIDEO ALTERATION SOFTWARE CAN MANUFACTURE VIDEOS OF A PRESIDENTIAL CANDIDATE WITH DEVASTATING IMPACTS ON THE CONFIDENCE OF VOTERS IN THE INFORMATION THEY INGEST.

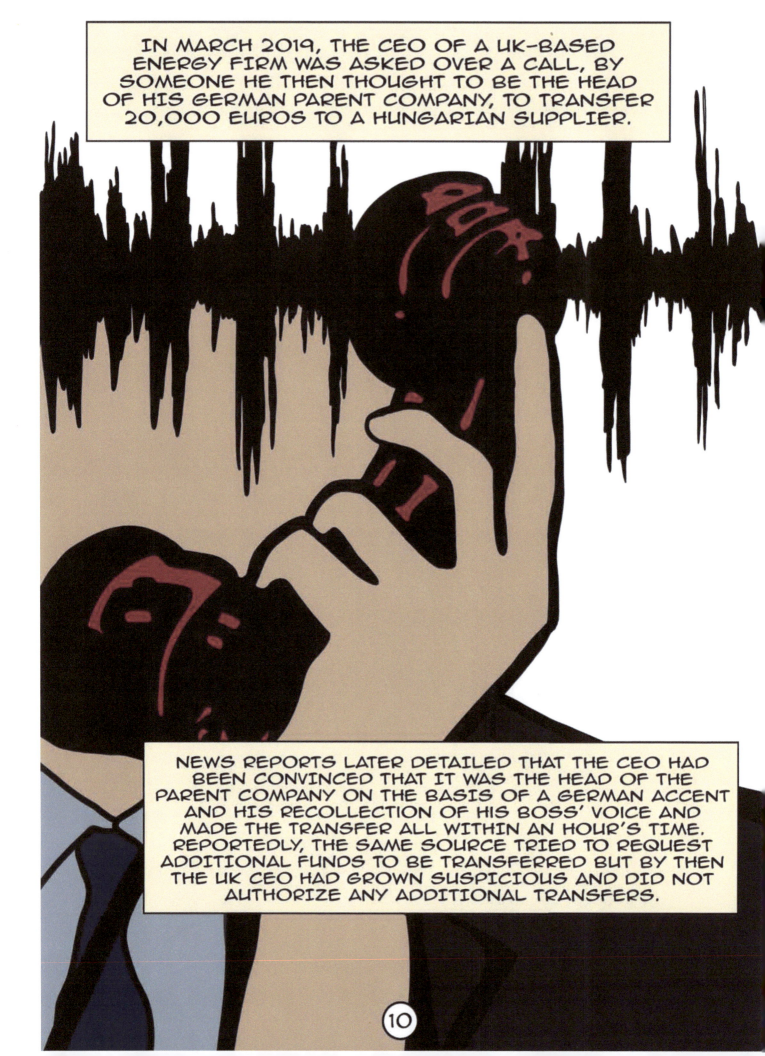

ACCORDING TO THE COMPANY'S INSURANCE COMPANY, FRAUDSTERS HAD LEVERAGED DEEPFAKE TECHNOLOGY AND ARTIFICIAL INTELLIGENCE TO CONSTRUCT A LIFE-LIKE RECORDING OF THE GERMAN GROUP HEAD'S VOICE. THE MONEY WAS SYPHONED OFF TO MEXICO AND CHANNELED TO OTHER ACCOUNTS.

THE FINANCIAL, POLITICAL, AND SOCIAL THREAT POSED BY DEEPFAKES (AND TODAY CHEAP FAKES), IS A VERY REAL RISK ABOUT WHICH SOCIETY AT LARGE NEEDS TO DEVELOP AWARENESS AND RESILIENCE.

The men who went to the moon to explore in peace

ONE TECHNIQUE FOR THE CREATION OF A DEEPFAKE VIDEO INVOLVES SWAPPING A PERSON'S FACE AND REPLACING IT WITH ANOTHER, USING A FACIAL RECOGNITION ALGORITHM AND A DEEP LEARNING COMPUTER NETWORK CALLED A VARIATIONAL AUTO-ENCODER (VAE).

VAES ARE TRAINED TO ENCODE IMAGES INTO SIMPLER LOW-DIMENSIONAL REPRESENTATIONS (THINK OF ZOOMING INTO A PICTURE TO SEE THE PIXEL) AND THEN DECODING THOSE REPRESENTATIONS BACK INTO IMAGES. FOR INSTANCE, IF YOU WANTED TO TRANSFORM A VIDEO OF ANYONE SPEAKING, YOU WOULD NEED TWO AUTO-ENCODERS. ONE TRAINED ON IMAGES OF THE SUBJECT'S FACE, AND ONE TRAINED ON IMAGES OF A WIDE RANGE OR DIVERSITY OF FACES.

THE IMAGES OF FACES USED FOR BOTH TRAINING SETS CAN BE CURATED BY APPLYING AN ALGORITHM FOR FACIAL RECOGNITION. THIS ALGORITHM IS ABLE TO CAPTURE VIDEO FRAMES FOR A DIVERSITY OF FACES IN VARIOUS NATURALLY OCCURRING POSES AND LIGHTING CONDITIONS.

TRAINING THE MACHINE IS WHY THE TERM MACHINE LEARNING IS USED TO DESCRIBE THIS PARTICULAR APPLICATION OF ARTIFICIAL INTELLIGENCE. ONCE THE MACHINE HAS LEARNED OR IS 'TRAINED,' IT IS THEN POSSIBLE TO COMBINE THE ENCODER TRAINED ON THE DIVERSE FACES WITH THE DECODER TRAINED ON THE SUBJECT'S FACE. THIS RESULTS IN THE SUBJECT'S FACE BEING ABLE TO BE PLACED ON SOMEONE ELSE'S BODY.

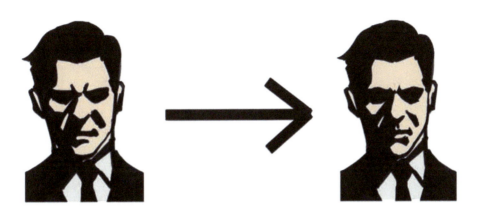

HOLLYWOOD HAS LEVERAGED DEEPFAKE TECHNOLOGY WITH GREAT SUCCESS, SUCH AS "GEMINI MAN" WHERE A MULTI-MILLION DOLLAR BUDGET PRODUCES A YOUNGER VERSION OF WILL SMITH THAT BATTLES WITH HIS CONTEMPORARY SELF. SIMILAR DE-AGING EFFECTS CAN BE SEEN IN "THE IRISHMAN" PRODUCED BY NETFLIX IN 2019.

WHILE THESE PRODUCTIONS SPARE NO EXPENSE AT BIG BUDGET DEEPFAKE WORK, ONE DOES NOT HAVE TO SEARCH TOO LONG ON YOUTUBE TO FIND PLENTY OF EXAMPLES OF CHEAP FAKES. ONE OF THE MOST PROMINENT EXAMPLES USES WILL SMITH'S FACE SUPERIMPOSED ON KEANU REEVES' FACE IN A SCENE FROM "THE MATRIX." THIS WAS CREATED BY A YOUTUBER USING A FREE SOFTWARE.

THIS IS EXCITING TECHNOLOGY FOR HOLLYWOOD BECAUSE IT ALLOWS FOR POSSIBILITIES LIKE RECREATING HISTORICAL VIDEOS SUCH AS PRESIDENT KENNEDY SPEAKING DURING THE CUBAN MISSILE CRISIS BUT USING AN ALTERNATIVE SCRIPT. MANY STUDIO EXECUTIVES SEE THE TECHNOLOGY AND ITS USE BECOMING MORE PERVASIVE IN THE COMING YEARS.

ANOTHER EXAMPLE WHERE THE TECHNOLOGY HAS FOUND A HOME, ONCE AGAIN IN THE ENTERTAINMENT INDUSTRY, IS IN GAMING.

GAME STUDIOS ARE CREATING "VOICE-SKINS" FOR USE IN ONLINE GAMES AND SOCIAL PLATFORMS. THE GAMING INDUSTRY IS LARGER THAN THE WORLD OF MOVIES AND BOOKS COMBINED AND THEREFORE THE COMMERCIAL POTENTIAL HERE IS LIKELY TO CONTINUE TO GATHER INTEREST.

THE GROWING INVENTORY OF ARTIFICIAL OR SYNTHETICALLY GENERATED VOICES CAN BE PURCHASED BY GAMING STUDIOS THAT ARE LOOKING TO OFFER A LEVEL OF REALISM IN THEIR GAMEPLAY THAT PREVIOUSLY COULD HAVE ONLY BEEN OFFERED BY REAL VOICE ACTORS.

will know that there is some corner of another world that is forever mankind

SOME OF THESE COMPANIES EMPLOY LARGE TEAMS THAT ARE SCANNING SOCIAL PLATFORMS AROUND THE WORLD AND IDENTIFYING THE EMERGENCE OF SUCH MEDIA, RECOGNIZING THAT SYNTHETIC CONTENT HAS THE POTENTIAL TO IMPACT ECONOMIES AND PEOPLE AROUND THE WORLD.

IT'S IMPORTANT FOR THE VOTING PUBLIC TO BE PARTICULARLY VIGILANT ABOUT THE CONTENT THEY SEE ON THE INTERNET, AND TO SEEK OUT TRUSTED SOURCES. THE CONSTANT CHURN OF USER-GENERATED CONTENT MIXED WITH PLANTED CHEAP FAKES IS A PARTICULAR AREA OF CONCERN FOR DEMOCRACIES AROUND THE WORLD THAT GRAPPLE WITH THE POTENTIAL INFLUENCE THIS TYPE OF MEDIA COULD HAVE IF VOTERS ARE FACED WITH ELECTION-RELATED DISINFORMATION.

WHILE MANY IN THE MEDIA ARE DOING GREAT WORK TO UNCLOAK AND REPORT ON DISINFORMATION AND EVEN IDENTIFY SPECIFIC DEEPFAKES, ALL OF THIS TALK ABOUT DISINFORMATION ALSO FEEDS WHAT IS REFERRED TO AS THE 'LIARS DIVIDEND.' THE PUBLIC BECOMES INCREASINGLY HYPERAWARE OF THE ISSUE AROUND THE ORIGIN OF CONTENT THAT THEY MAY EVEN START TO DOUBT THE VERACITY OF LEGITIMATE VIDEOS AND MEDIA ON THE INTERNET.

Goodnight

19

A FEW MONTHS EARLIER, MOSCOW, RUSSIA

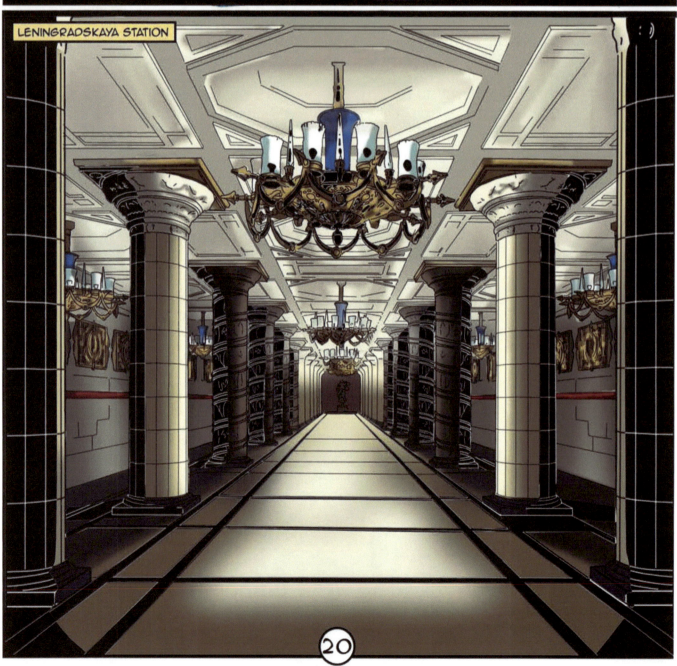

LENINGRADSKAYA STATION

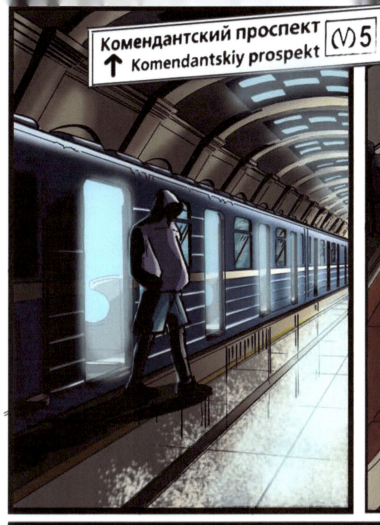

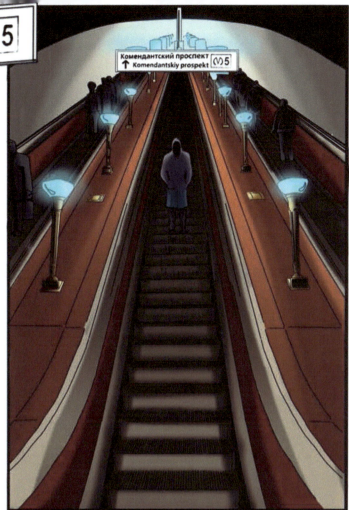

DING!

SECRET HOTEL SERVER ROOM
AND OPERATIONS CENTER

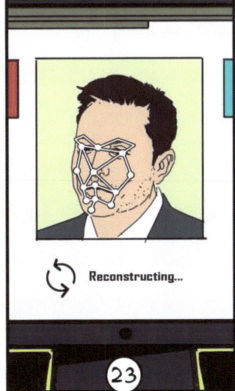

Reconstructing...

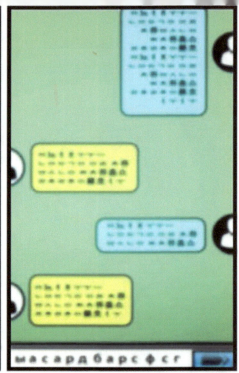

*TRANSLATED FROM RUSSIAN

<THAT IS THE NEXT PHASE FOR OUR DEEPFAKE CAMPAIGN.>

<WE MUST USE THE LATEST ALGORITHM AS IT HAS PERFECTED TEMPORAL STABILITY FOR HIGH-RESOLUTION VIDEOS. THIS WILL TAKE US TO THE NEXT LEVEL WITH HOW REAL THIS WILL SEEM TO THE AMERICANS.>

<THAT'S COOL. ARE WE THE FIRST TO DO THIS?>

<WE ARE ONLY THE SECOND TEAM IN THE WORLD TO HAVE PERFECTED THE ALGO THANKS TO THE GOOD WORK OF ZERO HERE! WE HAVE FULLY AUTOMATIC NEURAL FACE SWAPPING IN IMAGES AND VIDEOS! AND AT A MEGAPIXEL LEVEL!>

<THE LEADERSHIP WANTS RESULTS! NOW, IF YOU WILL EXCUSE ME, I NEED TO CHECK ON THE PRODUCTION MYSELF.>

АУДИО СТУДИЯ

<AUDIO STUDIO>

24

WEST AFRICA

VROOOOOM!

26

NUNEWZ OFFICE

Pay by Phone

PLEASE MAKE YOURSELF COMFORTABLE. CAN I GET YOU SOMETHING TO DRINK? WATER?

WE ARE VERY IMPRESSED WITH YOUR RESUME.

I AM GOOD FOR NOW, THANK YOU.

REALLY APPRECIATE THE OPPORTUNITY TO INTERVIEW HERE.

SO TELL ME A LITTLE ABOUT YOUR EXPERIENCE WITH CONTENT CREATION ON SOCIAL MEDIA.

WELL... I DID SOME WORK AROUND THE EBOLA VIRUS IN AFRICA LAST YEAR THROUGH SOME FREELANCING PLATFORMS.

VERY NICE. TELL ME, COULD YOU WRITE SOMETHING RIGHT NOW FOR ME? IN AMERICAN ENGLISH?

I COULD, YES.

GOOD. I WANT YOU TO WRITE A PIECE ON "CORRUPTION AT THE HIGHEST LEVELS" IN THE UNITED STATES. I WANT YOU TO THINK "SENATORS AND SENIOR OFFICIALS."

YES, BUT WHY WOULD THAT NEED A CAMPAIGN FROM THE U.S.?

IT'S A FOCUS RIGHT NOW IN THE STATES. WE HAVE AN INTEREST IN OUTING INJUSTICE. JUST LET ME SEE WHAT YOU CAN DO.

28

THIS IS YOUR STATION. MAKE SURE YOU SHOW ME HOW MANY POSTS AND WHAT ENGAGEMENT YOU GET DAILY IN A STATUS REPORT.

HALF AN HOUR LATER, AFTER A DEBRIEF WITH A NEW MANAGER...

ISAAC HERE WILL SHOW YOU HOW TO USE THE REPORTING SYSTEM. OUR FOUNDERS LIKE TO SEE DAILY RESULTS.

HAH..HI...

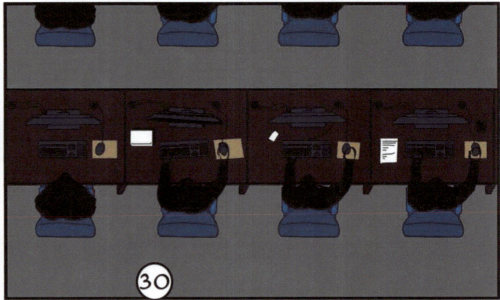

MEANWHILE IN WESTERN EUROPE...

ICHTECH OFFICES

PING

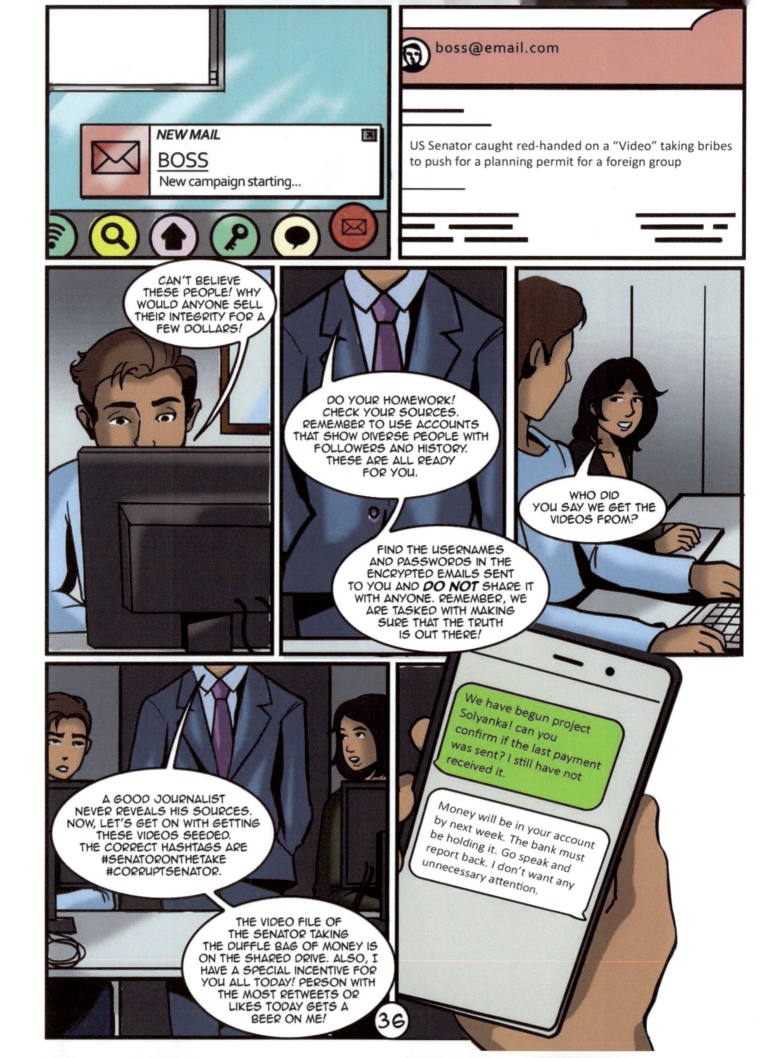

IT'S A BIT RISKY TO MEET UP SO SOON AND INTRODUCE THE IDEA OF SYMOUS, BUT WE DON'T SEEM TO HAVE MUCH TIME WITH THE CLOCK ON THE ELECTION TICKING!

Rachel
This Single0 guy is really getting on my nerves!

Andre
I'm seriously worried about how real it looks and the potential for this to go viral.

Rachel
I can't believe that no one else is calling these bogus videos out!

Andre
All bogus! None of that is true...

Rachel
I'm going to report this to the social media platform!

Andre
Let's hope they take the videos down.

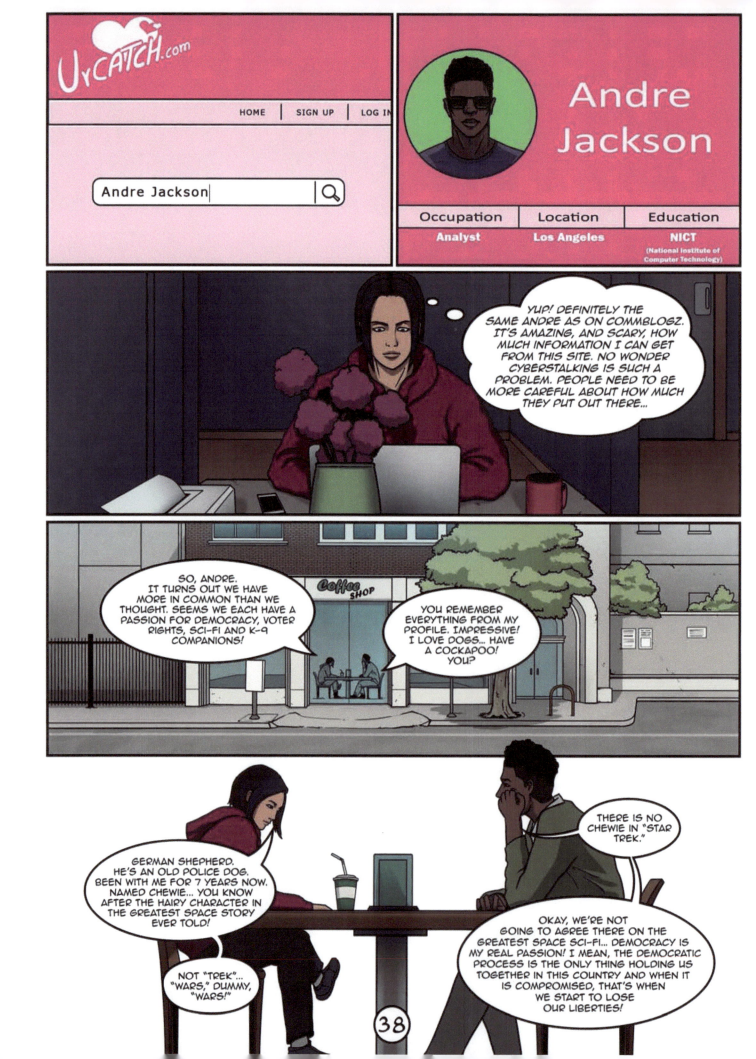

ALRIGHT. I'M IN! THIS BETTER BE LEGIT, AIDEN.

DO YOU HAVE A VALID PASSPORT?

TOTALLY. WHAT'S THE PLAN?

WE ARE GOING ON A LITTLE TRIP

WHERE ARE WE HEADED? CANADA?

HAH! NICE ONE!

43

SOMEWHERE OVER U.S. AIRSPACE CROSSING A STATE BORDER...

YOU OKAY?

I AM NOT A GOOD FLIER. DID I FORGET TO MENTION THAT? SODA SEEMS TO HELP.

YES! GLAD TO SEE THAT YOU ARE AS SHARP AS EVER DESPITE THE FLIGHT SICKNESS! GOT A BARF BAG READY?

THE IDEA IS TO GET IN AND UNDERSTAND IF THE TEAMS THERE KNOW WHAT THEY ARE ACTUALLY DOING AND GET A FEEL FOR WHO THEY ARE COMMUNICATING WITH.

OKAY, SO YOU ARE SAYING THAT WE ARE PRETENDING TO BE INVESTORS INTERESTED IN PUTTING MONEY INTO A SOCIAL MEDIA STARTUP WHICH IS A FRONT FOR A TROLL FARM?

WE SUSPECT THE PLACE IS BEING RUN OUT OF MOSCOW. AND YOU REMEMBER THAT TROLL YOU WERE SO UPSET ABOUT? THE ONE WHO POSTED THE DEEPFAKE? MR. ZERO... ONE OF THOSE PEOPLE IS THAT TROLL.

I THOUGHT THAT GUY WAS FROM NORTH KOREA?!

FIRST, IT MAY NOT BE A GUY. TAKE A LOOK AT ME FOR INSTANCE. PLENTY OF US ARE FEMALE HACKERS! SECOND, IT'S NEVER AS SIMPLE AS WYSIWYG (WHAT YOU SEE IS WHAT YOU GET) IN THIS SPACE.

46

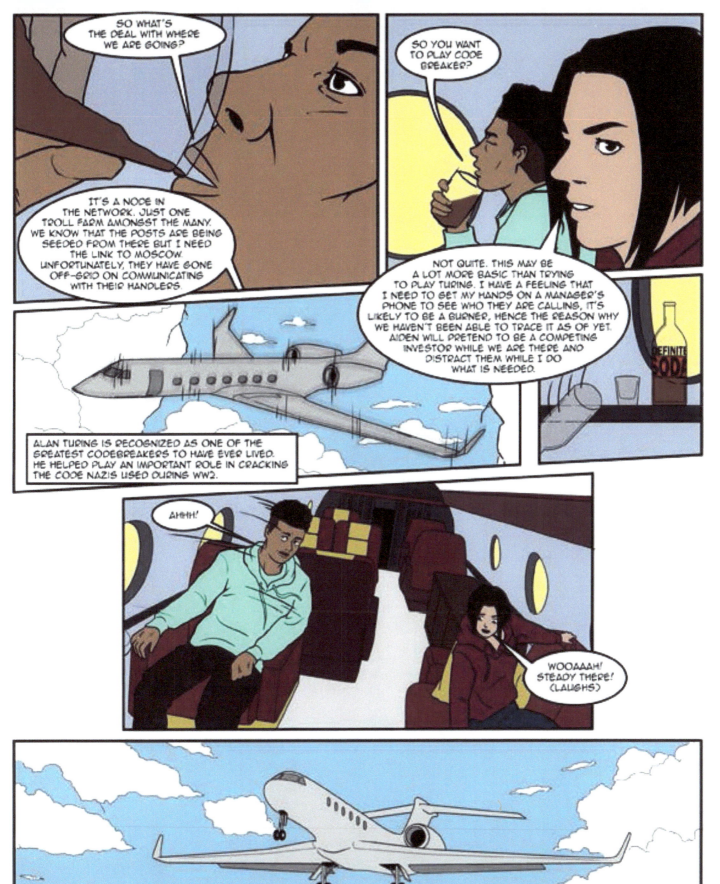

PRIVATE AIRFIELD OUTSIDE EUROPEAN CITY CENTER

47

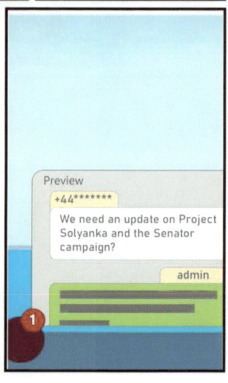

48

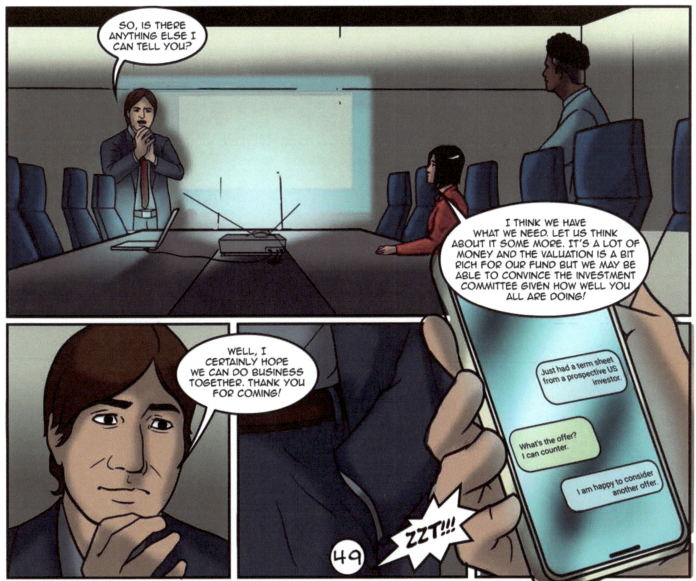

49

GOTCHA! PROOF IN HAND, FINALLY!

To HQ

Rachel
I saw this number pop up on his screen, could you trace it for me? I think this might be what we need +44 ••••••••

RACHEL TERMINAL V 1.5

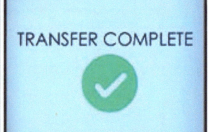

TRANSFER COMPLETE

AN HOUR LATER, BACK AT THE AIRSTRIP.

BRO! IT'S BEEN AGES!

YES, IT HAS.

HAVE FAITH, GENTLEMEN. WE HAVE THIS UNDER CONTROL BUT IT'S FAR FROM OVER!

GLAD TO SEE YOU ARE STILL GREAT AT GETTING US BOTH IN OVER OUR HEADS.

PRIVATE AIRSTRIP, OUTSKIRTS OF WEST AFRICAN CITY

WELCOME! WE HAVE BEEN EXPECTING YOU!

ANDREW PULLS OUT ALL THE PROTOCOL STOPS. DID I TELL YOU THAT HE KNOWS THE PRESIDENT PERSONALLY?

WE HAVE A RAID PARTY READY AND A COURT-MANDATED SEARCH WARRANT IN HAND! THANKS FOR THE TIP-OFF.

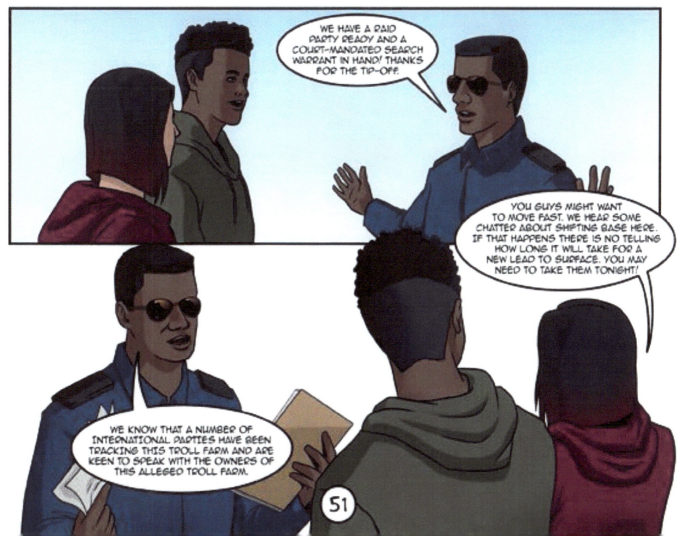

YOU GUYS MIGHT WANT TO MOVE FAST. WE HEAR SOME CHATTER ABOUT SHIFTING BASE HERE. IF THAT HAPPENS THERE IS NO TELLING HOW LONG IT WILL TAKE FOR A NEW LEAD TO SURFACE. YOU MAY NEED TO TAKE THEM TONIGHT!

WE KNOW THAT A NUMBER OF INTERNATIONAL PARTIES HAVE BEEN TRACKING THIS TROLL FARM AND ARE KEEN TO SPEAK WITH THE OWNERS OF THIS ALLEGED TROLL FARM.

51

I ALMOST FEEL BAD FOR THEM. DO YOU THINK THEY KNEW WHAT THEY WERE DOING?

THE NEXT MORNING...

HOW COULD THEY NOT? I MEAN, THEY WERE MANUFACTURING PROPAGANDA. IT'S PRETTY OBVIOUS ISN'T IT?

I'M NOT SO SURE. MAYBE, FROM THEIR PERSPECTIVE, THEY WERE MAKING A DIFFERENCE. YOU NEVER KNOW WHO WAS COMPLICIT AND WHO JUST GOT CAUGHT UP IN ALL OF THIS.

54

LATER THE SAME DAY, OUTSIDE THE NUNEWZ OFFICE.

THIS MAKES NO SENSE! THEY WERE ALL HERE JUST A FEW DAYS BACK! I SHOULD HAVE KNOWN, IT JUST SEEMED TOO GOOD TO BE TRUE.

Under Government Investigation

Business Closed Until Further Notice

The number you are calling is unavailable...

I BELIEVE SOME CONGRATULATIONS ARE IN ORDER! WELL DONE EVERYONE!

OUR DATA TEAMS HAVE REPORTED THAT THE TAKEDOWN OF THOSE INTERNATIONAL TROLL FARMS HAS RESULTED IN A DRAMATIC DECREASE IN THE NUMBER OF INCIDENTS RELATING TO DISINFORMATION ONLINE. IT'S TRENDING IN THE RIGHT DIRECTION AND WE HAVE A LOT TO BE PROUD OF AHEAD OF THE ELECTION. BUT WE MUST NOT LET DOWN OUR GUARD.

I AM ALREADY HEARING RUMBLINGS OF ACTIVITY BY DISINFORMATION CELLS IN OTHER PARTS OF ASIA. THESE GUYS ARE NIMBLE.

THANKS MR. CHAIRMAN. LET'S JUST SAY ITS A "TEAM SPORT." NOW ANDRE CAN GO BACK TO THAT STOREFRONT HE CALLS AN OFFICE AND LET THE "PROFESSIONALS" DEAL WITH THE NEXT CHALLENGE.

HEY... WATCH IT! OUR LITTLE STOREFRONT PUNCHES WELL ABOVE OUR WEIGHT CLASS. ON A SERIOUS NOTE, THANK YOU FOR TAKING ME ALONG ON THE JOURNEY. I HAVE LEARNED SO MUCH! IT'S GREAT TO BE A PART OF SYMOUS.

WE ARE JUST GETTING STARTED ANDRE. AS WE HEAD INTO THE FINAL WEEKS AHEAD OF THE BIG ELECTION DAY, REST ASSURED THAT WE WILL BE CALLING ON YOU AGAIN SHOULD SOMETHING SURFACE.

57

CREDITS

STORY BY

Farid Haque, Clint Watts

ART DIRECTION

Farid Haque, Annas Dar,
J. Nino Galenzoga

ILLUSTRATORS

J. Nino Galenzoga, Annas Dar,
Joel Santiago

COLORISTS

Mona S, Patricia Beja,
Joel Santiago

LETTERING

Haroon M, Komal N,
Patricia Beja

EDITOR

Tolly M.

SCRIPTWRITERS

Michael Gianfrancesco, Kabir Sabharwal

The Cybersecurity and Infrastructure Security Agency (CISA) produced this graphic novel to highlight tactics used by foreign government-backed disinformation campaigns that seek to disrupt American life and the infrastructure that underlies it. CISA's publication of information materials about this issue are intended for public awareness, and are not intended to restrict, diminish, or demean any person's right to hold and express any opinion or belief, including opinions or beliefs that align with those of a foreign government, are expressed by a foreign government-backed campaign, or dissent from the majority.

CISA celebrates the First Amendment rights of all U.S. persons without restriction. CISA doesn't endorse any products, services, institutions, or conduct outside of our authority that have been included in this story. While based on actual nation-state adversary activity, the story and all names, characters, organizations, and incidents portrayed in this production are fictitious.

NOTES FROM CISA

Disinformation is an existential threat to the United States, our democratic way of life, and the infrastructure on which it relies. The Resilience Series (of which this is the first title) uses the graphic novel format to communicate the dangers and risks associated with dis- and mis- information through fictional stories that are inspired by real-world events.

The Resilience Series graphic novels were commissioned by the Cybersecurity and Infrastructure Security Agency (CISA) to share information to illustrate:

- Foreign actors are trying to influence U.S. security, economy, and politics through the malicious use of online media to create and amplify disinformation.

- While the strategy of using inaccurate information to weaken and divide a society is not new, the internet and social media allow disinformation to spread more quickly than it has in the past.

- Deepfakes, bots, and troll farms are just some of the emerging techniques for creating and spreading disinformation.

CISA encourages everyone to consume information with care. Practicing media literacy – including verifying sources, seeking alternative viewpoints, and finding trusted sources of information – is the most effective strategy in limiting the effect of disinformation.

For more information and further reading about disinformation, please visit the Countering Foreign Influence Task Force webpage, www.cisa.gov/cfi-task-force.

BIBLIOGRAPHY

Page 8
C. Bregler and others. "Video Rewrite: Driving Visual Speech With Audio." 1997
www2.eecs.berkeley.edu/Research/Projects/CS/vision/human/bregler-sig97.pdf

Page 9, 11, 13, 15, 17, 19
www.news.mit.edu/2020/mit-tackles-misinformation-in-event-of-moon-disaster-0720

Page 15
J. Naruniec and others. "High-Resolution Neural Face Swapping for Visual Effects." 2020
s3.amazonaws.com/disney-research-data/wp-content/uploads/2020/06/18013325/High-Resolution-Neural-Face-Swapping-for-Visual-Effects.pdf

Page 19
R. Chesney and D. Citron. "Deepfakes and the New Disinformation War." 2019
www.foreignaffairs.com/articles/world/2018-12-11/deepfakes-and-new-disinformation-war